BENJAMIN NETANYAHU: Leading the Way for Israel

VOICES FROM ISRAEL

Elisa Silverman

D0931841

Mitchell Lane
PUBLISHERS
P.O. Box 196
Hockessin, Delaware 19707

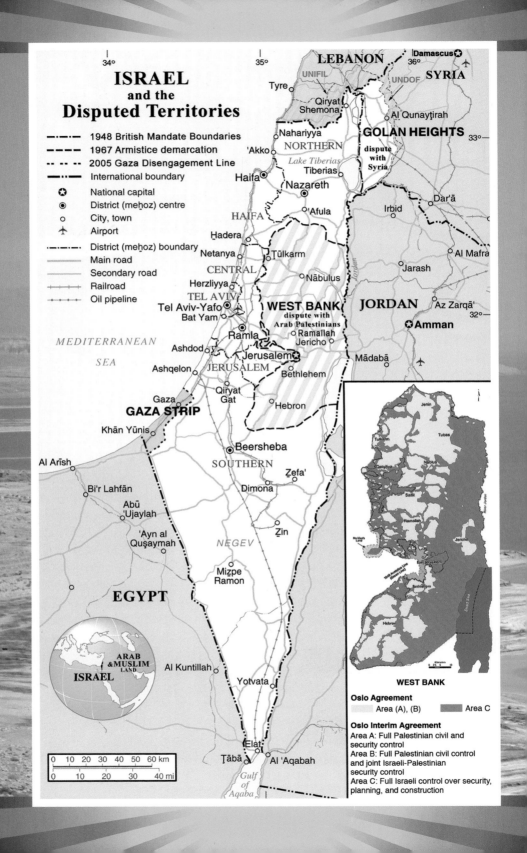

ISRAEL
and the
Disputed Territories

1948 British Mandate Boundaries
1967 Armistice demarcation
2005 Gaza Disengagement Line
International boundary

National capital
District (meḥoz) centre
City, town
Airport

District (meḥoz) boundary
Main road
Secondary road
Railroad
Oil pipeline

34°   35°   36°

LEBANON

Damascus ✪

SYRIA

UNIFIL   UNDOF

Tyre
Qiryat Shemona
Al Qunayṭirah
GOLAN HEIGHTS
Nahariyya
'Akko   NORTHERN   dispute with Syria
Lake Tiberias
Haifa   Tiberias   33°
Nazareth   Dar'ā
Afula   Irbid
HAIFA
Ḥadera   Al Mafra
Netanya   Tūlkarm   Jarash
CENTRAL   Nābulus
Herzliyya   Jordan
TEL AVIV   WEST BANK   JORDAN   Az Zarqā'
Tel Aviv-Yafo   dispute with   32°
Bat Yam   Arab Palestinians   ✪ Amman
Ramla   Ramallah
Ashdod   Jericho   Mādabā
MEDITERRANEAN   Jerusalem
SEA   JERUSALEM
Ashqelon   Bethlehem
Qiryat Gat
Gaza   Hebron
GAZA STRIP
Khān Yūnis
Al Arīsh   Beersheba
SOUTHERN   Zefa'
Bi'r Lahfān   Dimona
Abū 'Ujaylah
'Ayn al Quṣaymah   Zin
NEGEV

Mizpe Ramon

EGYPT

ISRAEL   ARAB & MUSLIM LAND

Al Kuntillah
Yotvata

Elat
Ṭābā   Al 'Aqabah
Gulf of Aqaba

0 10 20 30 40 50 60 km
0 10 20 30 40 mi

WEST BANK

Jenin
Tubas
Tulkarm
Nablus
Qalqiliya
Salfit
No Man's Land   Ramallah
Tel Aviv-Jerusalem (Green Line)   Jericho
East Jerusalem
Bethlehem
Hebron   Dead Sea

0 2.5 5   10
Kilometers

Oslo Agreement

Area (A), (B)   Area C

Oslo Interim Agreement
Area A: Full Palestinian civil and security control
Area B: Full Palestinian civil control and joint Israeli-Palestinian security control
Area C: Full Israeli control over security, planning, and construction

Set 1
Benjamin Netanyahu

The Experience of Israel: Sights and Cities

I Am Israeli: The Children of Israel

Returning Home: Journeys to Israel

Working Together: Economy, Technology, and Careers in Israel

Set 2
Americans in the Holy Land

Culture, Customs, and Celebrations in Israel

Israel and the Arab World

Israel: Holy Land to Many

Israel: Stories of Conflict and Resolution, Love and Death

Mitchell Lane
PUBLISHERS

Printing   1   2   3   4   5   6   7   8   9

Library of Congress Cataloging-in-Publication Data
Silverman, Elisa, author.
 Benjamin Netanyahu : leading the way for Israel / by Elisa Silverman.
   pages cm. — (Voice from israel)
 Includes bibliographical references and index.
 Summary: "Israel's youngest prime minister, as well as its longest serving prime minister, with the exception of Israel's first prime minister, David Ben-Gurion. Netanyahu has puzzled and surprised both his supporters and critics. He has experienced success, failure, and then success again. Through it all, Netanyahu has consistently fought for a strong Israel—militarily, politically, and economically. Netanyahu was born into an actively Zionist family whose own history mirrors that of Israel, her strengths and her struggles. A son, brother, scholar, soldier, and politician--each of these roles have shaped the leader Bibi is today"—Provided by publisher.
 ISBN 978-1-61228-680-8 (library bound)
1. Netanyahu, Binyamin. 2. Prime ministers—Israel—Biography—Juvenile literature. 3. Israel—Politics and government—1993—Juvenile literature. I. Title.
 DS126.6.N48S55 2015
 956.9405'4092—dc23
 [B]
                                                                        2015005675
eBook ISBN: 978-1-61228-689-1

ABOUT THE COVER: Prime Minister Benjamin Netanyahu stands in front of Israel's official state emblem, which shows two olive branches symbolizing peace surrounding a seven-branched menorah. The seven-branched menorah has been a symbol of the Jewish nation since the First Temple stood in Jerusalem (c. 1000–586 BCE).

PUBLISHER'S NOTE: This story is based on the author's extensive research and knowledge of Israel, which she believes to be accurate. Documentation of such research is contained on pp. 59–61.

The Internet sites referenced herein were active as of the publication date. Due to the fleeting nature of some web sites, we cannot guarantee they will all be active when you are reading this book.

To reflect current usage, we have chosen to use the secular era designations BCE ("before the common era") and CE ("of the common era") instead of the traditional designations BC ("before Christ") and AD (*anno Domini,* "in the year of the Lord").

PRONUNCIATION NOTE: The author has included pronunciations for many of the Hebrew words in this book. In these pronunciations, the letters "ch" are not pronounced like the "ch" in "children." Instead, the letters "ch" represent the Hebrew letter chet, which sounds like a "kh" or hard "h" sound, similar to the "ch" in "Loch Ness Monster."

PBP

CONTENTS

BOLD words in the text can be found in the glossary.

Introduction

When Benjamin Netanyahu (neh-tahn-YAH-hoo) was just a teenager, he used to wait by the mailbox in front of his home in Cheltenham, Pennsylvania. His older brother, Yonatan (Yoni or Jonathan), was back in Israel serving in the Israel Defense Force (IDF). "Bibi" (Netanyahu's nickname since he was a child) and his brother were very close, even inseparable, except by geography. Yoni wrote often and Bibi eagerly waited for those letters with news from his homeland. The year was 1963 and Yoni was the most recent Netanyahu to join the fight for Israel. Indeed the history of the Netanyahu family relates directly to the history of the state of Israel itself.

The modern state of Israel was established on May 14, 1948. The political **Zionist** movement, which promoted the idea that a new Jewish state should be created on the ancient Jewish homeland, had sprung to life just fifty years earlier. Rabbi Natan Mileikowsky (mee-lay-COW-ski), Netanyahu's grandfather, was an active member of that struggle. He was a popular speaker and traveled across three continents encouraging Jews to support the establishment of a Jewish state. His grandson would also become well known for his speaking skills on behalf of Israel. The rabbi wrote often on the issue, sometimes under the name "Netanyahu." Rabbi Mileikowsky's own son and Netanyahu's father, Benzion (ben-TZI-yown), which means "son of Zion" in Hebrew, decided to officially change the family name to "Netanyahu." The name "Netanyahu" means "God's gift" in Hebrew—a meaning some of Netanyahu's critics say he takes too literally in his view of himself as defender of the Jewish nation.

Rabbi Mileikowsky immigrated with his family in 1920 to Mandatory Palestine—a region in the Middle East under British control. However, he soon left to travel again throughout Europe and the United States to raise funds and awareness for the Zionist movement. This would be a pattern often repeated by the Netanyahu family. Fiercely committed to Israel, they are active participants in the struggle within its borders; however, they have also left Israel many times to fight for its survival from abroad. Benzion Netanyahu, who had lived in Mandatory Palestine since he was ten years old, left for the United States in 1940. He had been selected to head the US offices of the Revisionist Zionist movement—a faction of a broader Zionist movement that wanted stronger political action and a Jewish state to be established on both sides of the Jordan River. He worked to gain American political support for the establishment of the modern state of Israel. He also wrote articles warning that millions of Jews may be killed if they couldn't be allowed to move from Europe to Mandatory Palestine.[1] This belief in a constant threat to Jewish security is another common theme seen over and over again within the Netanyahu family and Israeli history.

Like his grandfather and father before him, Benjamin Netanyahu would also temporarily move to the United States in order to support Israel. Even before he became an official representative of the Jewish state, Netanyahu organized conferences to address the threat of terrorism to Israel and the world. Eventually, Netanyahu would go on to become Israel's youngest prime minister, its longest-serving prime minister since founding father David Ben-Gurion, and its first prime minister to be born in the modern state of Israel. From his days in Pennsylvania waiting for letters from his brother to his current place as Israel's prime minister, Netanyahu has been influenced by his family's history, its strengths and tragedies, and the history of his nation.

A young Bibi (on the right) hangs out on the steps with a friend in front of his family's Jerusalem home. (Inset) Netanyahu's high school yearbook photo.

CHAPTER 1
Growing Up Netanyahu

Like many children, Netanyahu got his nickname "Bibi" from his siblings. He was the middle child between two brothers, Yonatan and Iddo. The boys had a cousin, also named Benjamin, who was already nicknamed "Bibi." As Netanyahu remembers it, "He [the cousin] was the big B.B. . . . I was the small B.B."[1] The nickname stuck. Even today as prime minister, he is called Bibi by friends and foes alike. Using childhood nicknames for politicians is common in Israel.

Netanyahu was born on October 21, 1949 in Tel Aviv, Israel. He was born in a highly educated, **secular** family. His mother Cela had studied law. His father Benzion was a widely acclaimed historian who specialized in the history of Jews in Spain. While Netanyahu was born in Tel Aviv, he was raised primarily in Jerusalem. He attended Henrietta Szold Elementary School. One of his teachers wrote in his sixth-grade student evaluation that Bibi was "friendly, disciplined, cheerful, brave, active and obedient."[2] A college professor of his would later use some similar words to describe him, "He was very bright. Organized. Strong. Powerful."[3]

Coming to America

In 1956 his father moved the family from Jerusalem to the Philadelphia suburb of Cheltenham, Pennsylvania. Benzion Netanyahu had taken a job as a professor at Dropsie College, where he had earned his degree. They stayed in Pennsylvania until 1958, when the family returned to Israel. They returned to Pennsylvania in 1963 when Netanyahu was fourteen years old. Netanyahu did well at Cheltenham High School, describing himself as both a nerd and a jock.[4] The other soldiers who served with Netanyahu in the IDF saw him much the same way. They remember him as mentally and physically strong, and very "straight-laced . . . 'a bit of a nerd.' "[5] During the time he lived in America, Netanyahu developed a great appreciation for

America. He also developed what would become one of his greatest assets in his political life—fluent English spoken in a perfect American accent.

As is common in Israeli culture, Netanyahu's family ties are strong. Today, Netanyahu is married to his third wife Sara, who is a psychologist. He has three children. His daughter Noa, from his first marriage, was born in 1978. He and his wife Sara have two sons together, Yair and Avner. His father, who lived until he

Netanyahu and his father consult texts at his father's house in Jerusalem on February 8, 2009, just two days before the election that would send Netanyahu back to the prime minister's office.

was 102 years old, was one of Netanyahu's strongest influences. His father died on April 30, 2012. Despite his duties to the state as prime minister, Netanyahu fulfilled his duties to his father by formally mourning his father's death for the full seven days after burial, in accordance with Jewish custom. His older brother Yonatan was also a great influence on Netanyahu's life. From both his father and his brother, Netanyahu gained the perspective at a young age that only a strong Israel could be a secure Israel. This attitude continues to guide Netanyahu.

Netanyahu, his wife Sara, and their two sons Yair and Avner, host guests for the first night of Chanukah in the Prime Minister's Office in 1996. Netanyahu lights a menorah, which holds a candle for each night of the eight-day festival. Chanukah celebrates the rededication of the Holy Temple in Jerusalem ca. 165 BCE, after the Jews recaptured it from the Syrian-Greek army.

YONATAN (YONI) NETANYAHU

Netanyahu's older brother Yoni fought in many of Israel's wars. Before he was thirty years old, he was a national hero. Many thought Yoni would enter politics, but he did not get the chance.

Yoni was killed on July 4, 1976 when he led an IDF commando force in rescuing more than one hundred hostages held by Palestinian and German terrorists at an airport in Entebbe, Uganda. As part of the raid, IDF soldiers tried to trick the Ugandan soldiers guarding the airport. They drove a black Mercedes, just like the one used by Uganda's leader. What they didn't know was that the Ugandan leader had recently gotten a white Mercedes—but the Ugandan soldiers knew.

A firefight broke out and the terrorists knew they were under attack. The IDF commando unit successfully freed all the hostages in less than fifty-three minutes. There was only one Israeli death—Yoni Netanyahu.

Yoni

Netanyahu couldn't eat for weeks after hearing of his brother's death. Yoni's influence on Netanyahu remains strong, and may have led him to politics. One of Netanyahu's advisers thinks "Bibi lives for two people, himself and Yoni."[6] Netanyahu wrote that Yoni's death "changed my life and directed it to its present course."[7]

Yoni's gravestone (with IDF logo in the upper right corner)

Netanyahu from his days as a member of the Sayeret Matkal, Israel's elite commando unit. Netanyahu served in the unit from 1968–1973, participating in many risky operations. Netanyahu nearly drowned during such a mission in Egypt in 1969.

A Scholar and A Soldier

A common crossroads for any teenager is when high school is ending and choices must be made. Go to college? Which college? Perhaps join the military? That was the crossroads Netanyahu faced during his last year of high school. He had been accepted to Yale University; however, it was also time for him to return to Israel and fulfill his military duty. He didn't even wait for his high school graduation ceremony. When the Six Day War began on June 5, 1967, he, along with many Israelis in the United States, rushed back to Israel. He was selected to join one of the IDF's most elite commando units, Sayeret Matkal. While Israeli law requires three years of military service from boys (the girls are required to serve two years), Netanyahu served for five years from 1967 through 1972. He returned to active duty during the **Yom Kippur** War in 1973. He was ultimately discharged from the IDF in 1973 with the rank of captain.

Operations Gift and Isotope

As a commando with Sayeret Matkal, Netanyahu participated in a number of dangerous missions for the IDF. Two of them were Operation Gift and Operation Isotope.

Operation Gift was a raid on the airport in Beirut, Lebanon. The operation was carried out on December 28, 1968 just two days after a Lebanon-based Palestinian terrorist group had attacked an El Al airplane (El Al is Israel's national airline). As part of the raid, the unit removed all the people found on board thirteen commercial airplanes operated by various Arab-owned companies, and then destroyed the planes.

Operation Isotope took place much closer to home. On May 8, 1972 a commercial flight going from Vienna to Tel Aviv was hijacked by four members of Black September, a Palestinian terrorist organization. The plane was landed at the Tel Aviv airport. The hijackers demanded that Israel release 315 Palestinians from Israeli prisons. Netanyahu was part of a sixteen-man unit that was led by his future political friend and competitor, Ehud Barak. As part of the operation, an IDF squad secretly disabled the plane and cut its tires. When the terrorists

Sabena Flight 571 was highjacked on May 8, 1972 by four members of the Black September Organization, the same Palestinian terror group that would kill 11 Israeli coaches and athletes during the Olympic games in Munich, Germany just four months later. One of the hostages died from injuries due to the firefight between the commandos and the terrorists. The two surviving terrorists were sentenced to life in prison, but were eventually released as part of a prisoner exchange ten years later.

Decades after Operation Isotope, Netanyahu and Barak team up once again. In 2011, now as Prime Minister Netanyahu and Defense Minister Barak, the men watch Israel's missile defense system in action.

were unable to operate the plan, the undercover Sayeret Matkal unit was sent in dressed as mechanics. The commandos stormed the plane to free the hostages. In less than ninety seconds, two of the terrorists were killed, the other two were captured, and their explosives were made useless. Netanyahu had minor injuries during the counter-attack.

Returning to America

When Netanyahu was released from his military duty, he returned to the United States to attend college. He had lost his acceptance to Yale, but that was not a problem. Instead, he attended the Massachusetts Institute of Technology (MIT), where he earned a Bachelor of Science (BS) degree in architecture in 1975. He had been taking a double course load from the start, so he also earned a master degree (MS) in management in 1976.

He was a twenty-three year old war veteran when he started college and he was used to hard work. As happened so often in his life, he was pulled back and forth between Israel and the United States while he was in school. A year into his studies at MIT, Israel suffered a surprise attack from a number of its Arab neighbors on October 6, 1973. It was Judaism's holiest day of the year—Yom Kippur. Netanyahu returned to Israel and the IDF for forty days to join the fight as the nation fought off the attack.

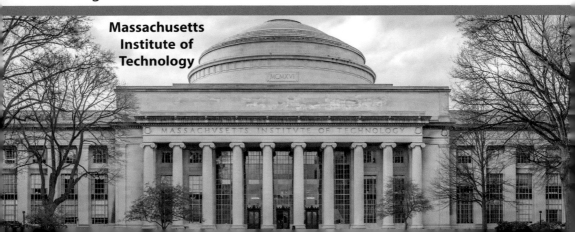

Massachusetts Institute of Technology

Lieutenant Benjamin Netanyahu at a ceremony on November 1, 1972, honoring the soldiers involved in freeing the hostages during Operation Isotope. Netanyahu is seen shaking the hand of Israeli president Zalman Shazar.

Back at MIT in November 1973, Netanyahu continued his studies. He co-authored his management thesis, called "Computerization and the Newspaper Industry." In it, he and his co-author Zeev Zurr predicted that technology advances would radically alter the traditional production process of the newspaper.[1] Netanyahu later authored several books about Israel, **Zionism**, and his family.

Even though he was studying for two degrees, Netanyahu decided to take some additional courses in political science. He was about to begin studying for an advanced degree in political science when he received the news of his brother Yonatan's death; he immediately returned to Israel.

He returned to the United States later that year, but he was no longer a student. From 1976–1978, Netanyahu worked at the Boston Consulting Group, where he first met future American presidential candidate and fellow employee, Mitt Romney. In 1978, he left to found and direct the Jonathan Institute (named for his brother), which is dedicated to exploring ways to fight terrorism. After two years at the institute, Netanyahu returned to Israel where he worked in the senior management of Israel's largest furniture manufacturer from 1980 to 1982.

Even though he was in the private business sector, Netanyahu organized the first of two international conferences in 1979, which was held in Jerusalem. The second conference he organized was held in Washington, DC, in 1984. The conferences were attended by influential political figures and discussed the need to fight terrorism and the governments that support it. Heading the institute and organizing the conferences were Netanyahu's first steps into public life. It is no coincidence that the institute and conferences were focused on Israel's security.

SAYERET MATKAL

Sayeret Matkal is the IDF's most elite special commando force. The unit, founded in 1957, was based on the British special forces unit, known as SAS. Sayeret Matkal even shares SAS's motto: "Who dares wins."

Sayeret Matkal sits in the IDF's Military Intelligence unit. It gathers and acts on intelligence primarily in the areas of the world where Israel's most dangerous enemies exist. Members of Sayeret Matkal go through grueling training. Its operations are demanding, daring, and clever. One former member explained, "Let's say there's a tank division that's going to attack Israel. The regular way would be to send another tank division to block it. The Sayeret Matkal way would be to send a unit and empty the tanks of gas, and win without firing a shot."[2]

Many of Israel's political, intelligence, and military leaders served in the Sayeret Matkal.

Sayeret Matkal soldiers

Netanyahu visits with Sorin Hershko, one of the Israeli soldiers wounded in the Entebbe raid, on July 2, 1986. Sorin was paralyzed due to injuries he suffered during the operation to free the hostages. Hershko is also a founder of LOTEM, an organization in Israel that helps make nature and hiking accessible to people with special needs.

CHAPTER 3
Entering Politics

As respectful as Netanyahu was of his father, he did defy him by becoming a politician. His father hated politicians and discouraged his son from becoming one. But what's done is done. So when Netanyahu was first elected prime minister, he turned to his father for advice. He recalls his father advising him that "what you need to lead a country is education . . . an understanding of history, the knowledge to be able to put things in perspective."[1]

Netanyahu's Perspective of the World
His family's history with Revisionist Zionism strongly shaped Netanyahu's own worldview. Revisionism, and followers like Netanyahu's father, believes the combination of territorial and military strength is the key to Jewish survival. Netanyahu also believes, as his father did, that **anti-Semitism** is inevitable, and that the Jewish people will always be in a continuing fight for survival.

The result of this view is that Netanyahu believes that his greatest responsibility as a leader of Israel is to protect the Jewish homeland. He presented his view of Zionism and Israel in his book *A Place Among the Nations*. In Hebrew, the title translates to "A Place Under the Sun," reflecting his commitment that Jews must have a physical homeland in order to be secure.

Netanyahu's focus on security explains many of his political positions. These include his view on trading land for peace with the Palestinians to his warnings against a nuclear Iran. Netanyahu is clear that he sees an Iran with nuclear weapons as Israel's and the world's greatest threat. Minimizing the Iranian threat is one of his primary goals.

First an Ambassador, then a Politician

When Moshe Arens, a family friend, was Israel's ambassador to the United States, he appointed Netanyahu his **Deputy Chief of Mission** in 1982. It was time for Netanyahu to return to America. Netanyahu was frequently interviewed on television in his role as representative of Israel in the United States. He spoke well and with an American accent, which made him a popular guest to present Israel's side of the complicated news coming from the Middle East. That was the beginning of his popularity, both in Israel and in the United States.

Due to his growing popularity and influence, he was appointed Israel's ambassador to the United Nations in 1984. He held that post until 1988 when he returned to Israel to become a member of Israel's parliament, called the *Knesset* (ki-NEH-set). He was voted in as a member of the right wing *Likud* (li-KOOD) party, a membership he still retains. At the same time, he was also appointed Deputy Foreign Minister. Prime Minister Yitzhak Shamir (yeetz-CHAK shah-MEER) appointed Netanyahu Deputy Prime Minister in 1991. As such, Netanyahu was a member of Israel's delegation to the Madrid Peace Conference in 1991. The conference was jointly sponsored by the United States and the Soviet Union. Its goal was to bring Israel together with representatives from different Arab countries to start a peace process. It was the first time that Israeli and Palestinian representatives sat together at a negotiating table.

Moshe Arens was first elected to the Knesset in 1974 as a member of the Likud party. He went on to serve Israel as its Defense Minister, Foreign Minister, and ambassador to the United States. Arens was a mentor of Netanyahu's and brought him into public life. While he would later oppose Netanyahu for leadership of the Likud party, he also supported Netanyahu's decision to address the US Congress in March 2015.

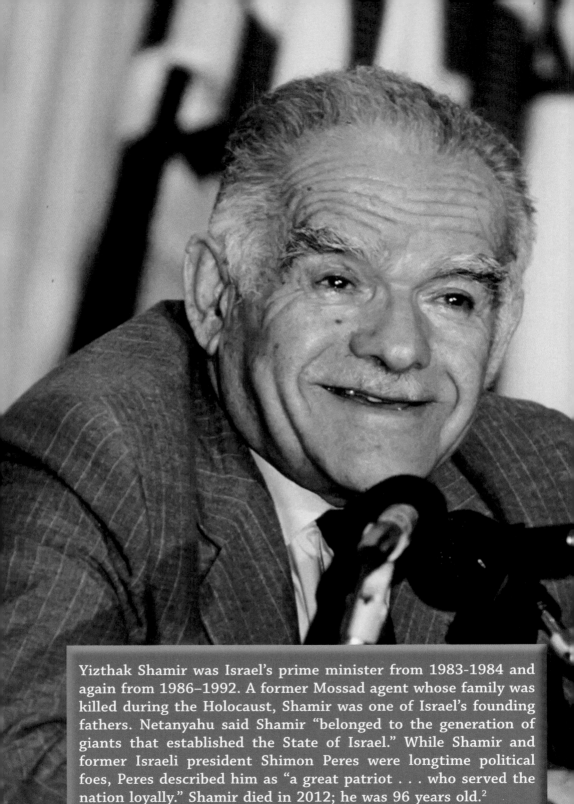

Yizthak Shamir was Israel's prime minister from 1983-1984 and again from 1986–1992. A former Mossad agent whose family was killed during the Holocaust, Shamir was one of Israel's founding fathers. Netanyahu said Shamir "belonged to the generation of giants that established the State of Israel." While Shamir and former Israeli president Shimon Peres were longtime political foes, Peres described him as "a great patriot . . . who served the nation loyally." Shamir died in 2012; he was 96 years old.[2]

Becoming a Leader

Netanyahu won the Likud primary to be the party's leader on March 25, 1993 with more than fifty-two percent of the vote. Being elected head of a political party is necessary before becoming prime minister, so that was an important step in Netanyahu's political career. However by that time, the Likud party had fallen out of power. Its rival from the left, the Labor party, led by Yitzhak Rabin (yeetz-CHAK Rah-BEEN) was in power.

While the leadership in Israel changed, the country continued the peace negotiations started at the Madrid Peace Conference. On September 13, 1993 Israel and the Palestinian Liberation Organization (PLO) signed the Oslo I Accords on the White House lawn in Washington, DC. The agreement allowed the transfer of land in the West Bank from Israeli to Palestinian control and democratic self-rule. In return for the Israelis giving up the land, the PLO promised to no longer use violence in its fight against Israel.

The Oslo I Accords were controversial. Netanyahu and other politicians spoke out strongly against them. They said the PLO and its leader had no intention of stopping their acts of violence against Israel. They also argued that even if the PLO stopped acting violently itself, it was not strong enough to prevent violence by other Palestinian groups. The result would be that Israel would lose land but gain no peace. There were protests in Israel against Oslo, at which many protesters presented Prime Minister Rabin as a villain and traitor for making the agreement.

While some Israelis were skeptical, others believed Oslo was a true opportunity for peace. There were also many rallies in Israel in support of the agreement. Many Israeli supporters of Rabin and Oslo harshly criticized Netanyahu and others on the right for protesting against Oslo. It was a tense time in

Israel as the divisions within Israeli society were quite ugly. Many Palestinians rejected Oslo too. Hezbollah (hez-buh-LAH), a terrorist group in Lebanon controlled by Iran, increased its attacks on Israel from the north.

On November 4, 1995, Prime Minister Rabin was assassinated by an Israeli Jew. One of the anti-Oslo protesters who saw Rabin as a traitor to Israel shot Rabin after he spoke at a peace rally in Tel Aviv. Israeli society was horrified that an Israeli Jew killed an Israeli prime minister. Increasing the painful and ugly mood in the country, some on the left blamed Netanyahu and his anti-Oslo speeches for the assassination. That turmoil was part of the background against which Netanyahu was first elected prime minister on May 29, 1996.

Rabin was assassinated near the Kings of Israel Square in Tel Aviv. The square has since been renamed Rabin Square. This memorial to Rabin is near the spot where he was killed. The Hebrew word in large graffiti is slicha (slee-CHAH), which literally means "forgiveness." Israelis use it to say "sorry" or "pardon me."

REVISIONIST ZIONISM (REVISIONISM)

Ze'ev Jabotinsky (jah-bow-TIN-skee) founded Revisionist Zionism, also called "Revisionism" in 1925. Jabotinsky had been active in the Zionist movement for over twenty years by the time he founded Revisionism. He felt a "revision" of the current approach of political Zionism was needed. The Revisionist movement wanted a clear and immediate declaration that Jews had a right to establish a Jewish state on the entire biblical land of Israel, spanning across both sides of the Jordan River.

Of course there were already many other people besides Jews living in the area, an issue that Jabontinsky addressed. He rejected the idea of removing Arabs from the land, but he also believed that Arabs and Jews couldn't live together as things were. He wrote that as long as Arabs have a hope of preventing a Jewish state, they would fight. His solution was to create an "iron wall" of military force that would eventually convince the Arabs that they could never get rid of the Jews. Only then, he reasoned, would Arabs be willing to make a peace deal. Revisionisms' critics, then and now, believe his approach is too militaristic.

Revisionism is seen as the birthplace of the political right in Israel and of Netanyahu's party, the Likud. The movement was largely opposed by the Labor Zionists, the forerunner to Israel's Labor party and the country's political left.

Ze'ev Jabotinsky (front row, center) with members of the Zionist youth group he founded, Betar (Tel Aviv, ca. 1928).

Netanyahu and a member of the Ethiopian community in Israel share a moment at a memorial service remembering the Ethiopian Jews who lost their lives trying to immigrate to Israel. From the 1980s until 2013, the Israeli government operated special flights from Africa bringing thousands of Ethiopian immigrants to Israel. Many Ethiopian Jews had to walk to Sudan in order to get to Israel, a dangerous journey during which many of them died.

Netanyahu's First Try

His winning percentage of the vote could hardly have been smaller for a victorious candidate. On May 29, 1996, Israelis elected Netanyahu with only 50.4 percent of the vote. His main rival was Shimon Peres from the Labor party. Peres had been foreign minister under Rabin and he believed strongly in Oslo. Netanyahu remained critical of the agreement, but he said during that campaign that if the PLO would keep its commitments under Oslo, so would Israel. He campaigned on the slogan "Peace with Security." His message was that he was the one leader who could make sure that Israel only took actions under Oslo that moved Israel toward peace without risking her security.

Fragile Government from the Start

Netanyahu's narrow victory was only one sign of his weakness in office. Peres' Labor party was the largest party in the Knesset. The Likud, which had often won more than forty of the one hundred twenty Knesset seats available, won only twenty-three this time. It could have had more, but in order to be the only candidate for prime minister on the right, Netanyahu made deals with two other potential candidates to keep them out of the race. In return, representatives from those other parties got seats in the Knesset instead of Likud members. It was a deal that left Netanyahu with angry members from his own party and a **coalition** over which he had little influence.

Netanyahu tried different ways to keep his political rivals in line. He brought powers normally belonging to the defense and finance ministries into the Prime Minister's Office. He appointed members to his cabinet from a wide range of parties, but this only lessened his ability to influence them. He threatened parties on the right that if they didn't support his policies, he would create a **national unity government** with the Labor party, which would leave them out of power. Those actions didn't strengthen his position. The results were that no one was happy and no one trusted him.

Making More Deals

During the campaign, Netanyahu had said that he would continue the Oslo process as long as the Palestinians continued to keep their promises under the agreement. While some criticized Netanyahu and his government for not keeping the peace process moving forward, others criticized him for giving away land without getting anything in return from the Palestinians.

On January 17, 1997, Israel and the PLO signed the Hebron Agreement. This agreement gave the **Palestinian Authority (PA)** control over eighty percent of the town of Hebron. It was the first time in Israel's history that it had given away any part of *Eretz Yisrael* (eh-RETZ yis-RAH-el), and one of Judaism's four holy cities at that. The agreement was originally negotiated under the Rabin government, but Netanyahu signed it. His supporters on the right were incensed. In order to get cabinet approval for another agreement shortly after Hebron, Netanyahu agreed to approve an increase of housing for Jews in East Jerusalem. He also limited the amount of land given to the Palestinians under that second agreement to much less than

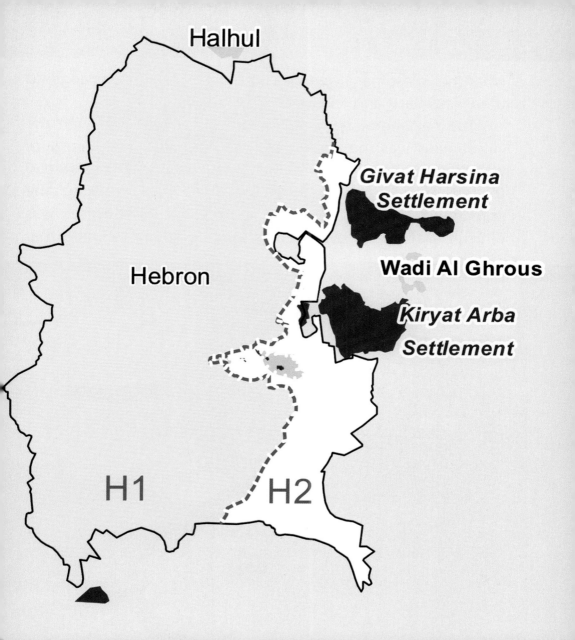

Halhul

Givat Harsina
Settlement

Wadi Al Ghrous

Hebron

Kiryat Arba

Settlement

H1

H2

As part of the Hebron Agreement, Israel withdrew its military from 80 percent of Hebron (area H1), leaving it to Palestinian control. The other 20 percent (area H2) remains under Israeli military administration and includes the Tomb of the Patriarchs, a site holy to both Jews and Muslims. The tomb is the burial site of biblical patriarchs and matriarchs: Abraham and Sarah, Isaac and Rebekah, and Jacob and Leah.

what the Palestinians wanted.[1] Both of those positions angered the Palestinians and left-wing Israelis.

The next agreement that Netanyahu negotiated with the Palestinians was the final straw. The Wye River Memorandum was signed October 23, 1998. In it, Netanyahu and Israel agreed to further withdrawals from the West Bank. Getting the agreement approved by his cabinet and the Knesset was difficult. Netanyahu eventually suspended Wye, claiming that

The Wye River Memorandum was named for the location of the negotiations. Here, Netanyahu and US president Bill Clinton discuss matters with Israel's ambassador to the United States, Zalman Shoval (far left) and Israel's defense minister Yitzhak Mordechai (second from left) on October 20, 1998 in Wye River, Maryland.

the PA wasn't meeting its obligations. Members of the PA and other Netanyahu critics made the same claim of Israel. As both the left and the right became more frustrated with Netanyahu, he asked the Labor party, which had the most seats in the Knesset, to join Likud in a national unity government. His goal was to stay on top of the **ruling coalition**. It didn't work.

Netanyahu's Defeat

At that point it seemed like everyone was mad at Netanyahu. His political allies weren't supporting him because he was giving land away and Israel wasn't getting any security in return. Palestinian violence had increased. The left wing, which had supported the agreements he made with the Palestinians, saw their opportunity to regain power. Average Israelis, whether on the right or left, generally shared the views their politicians had of Netanyahu.

In December 1998 Netanyahu announced the upcoming elections. Netanyahu's own mentor Moshe Arens challenged him for leadership of the Likud. Politicians and candidates from the right, center, and left wings of Israeli politics, as well as the media, all made Netanyahu the main issue of the campaign.

He had been elected as Israel's youngest prime minister when he was forty-six years old. Israel had never before had a prime minister under the age of sixty. Israel is a country where the Hebrew word for "old person"—zakayn (zah-KANE) is the same word for "wise person." Many people felt that it was obvious that he was too young and too inexperienced to handle the complex and serious demands of being an Israeli prime minister. Calling Netanyahu too young and inexperienced were the nicest things that his opponents had to say about him during that campaign. His honesty, credibility, and leadership were all questioned, often in ugly language.[2]

Netanyahu's main rival was his former commander Ehud Barak, now the leader of the Labor party. Barak used the slogan "One Israel," in part to contrast his call for national unity against Netanyahu's reputation for divisiveness. On May 17, 1999, Barak handily defeated Netanyahu. Barak was elected prime minister of Israel with more than fifty-six percent of the votes.

Ehud Barak was prime minister from 1999-2001. He had earlier served many Labor party prime ministers in various ministerial positions. He would go on to serve as Minister of Defense and deputy prime minister under Netanyahu from 2009-2013. Barak left politics in 2013.

AMERICAN-STYLE ELECTIONS

Netanyahu was the first prime minister to be elected directly by the Israeli people. Before his election, Israelis only voted for a political party, not a politician. After the election, the president would ask a Knesset member, usually the leader of the party that received the highest percentage of votes, to form a government. That party leader then became prime minister—if he or she could form a ruling coalition.

The Knesset voted in 1992 to have the Israeli people vote directly for the prime minister. They called it "American-style elections." They hoped it would mean more stable government since the prime minister couldn't be brought down because of fights in the coalition or Knesset.

The first direct election was held in 1996. Netanyahu won. However, the Labor party, Likud's main political rival, won the highest percentage of the popular vote. So the party with power in the Knesset was not the prime minister's party, which made Netanyahu a prime minister with very little political power. That was a new situation for Israel.

Prime ministers who were directly elected didn't have enough power in the Knesset to get laws passed. Their weakness resulted in Israel having two more elections for prime minister over the next five years. Those "American-style" elections did not bring stability, but only politically weak prime ministers. As a result, Israel went back to the old system in 2003.

An Israeli man is helped by his granddaughter as he votes in the 2003 election.

In 2004, Prime Minister Ariel Sharon and Finance Minister Netanyahu watch in the Knesset chamber as Knesset members vote down six no-confidence motions. No-confidence motions are used in parliamentary systems by members opposed to the government to express their lack of confidence in the majority's ability to govern. In this instance, opponents to Sharon and Netanyahu were upset over the country's economy.

Returning to Politics

After a bruising campaign that seemed to focus mostly on Netanyahu's personal and political failings, could any politician make a comeback? It was easy to assume that public life for Netanyahu was done. A short nineteen months later in December 2000, Barak resigned as prime minister and Netanyahu was again on top of Israeli opinion polls.[1]

Israel had made another agreement with the PA under Barak. That agreement was intended to restart Wye by setting up a timeline for each side to fulfill its duties. Instead, violence in the West Bank and terror attacks within Israel were increasing, causing Israelis to lose faith in the Oslo peace process. The need to feel more secure in Israel pushed Israeli voters back to the right—but they weren't quite ready for Netanyahu again, not yet. Netanyahu decided not to run for prime minister when Barak resigned and called for a special election. On February 6, 2001, the new head of the Likud, Ariel Sharon (AIR-ee-el Sha-RONE), beat Barak in a landslide. Sharon became prime minister with sixty-two percent of the vote.[2]

The Comeback
Netanyahu returned, for the most part, to private life after he lost the election in 1999. He advised companies in Israel's hi-tech sector. He was also invited to give speeches in Israel, the United States, and elsewhere. In November 2002, Netanyahu became a politician again. Sharon appointed Netanyahu to be

Foreign Minister. By that time the two men already had a complicated relationship as political rivals in the same party. In fact, Sharon had been Netanyahu's foreign minister and had led the Wye negotiations on behalf of Israel.

When Sharon was re-elected prime minister in January 2003, he appointed Netanyahu as his Finance Minister. Many saw this as a slap in the face to Netanyahu. Due in large part to the ongoing violence in the region, Israel was in a terrible economic condition. Sharon expected Netanyahu to be out of the way in the Finance Ministry. Before accepting the position, Netanyahu negotiated for broad powers to manage the country's finances. Sharon, who was more focused on the peace process and not interested in economics, agreed.

Life as a Finance Minister

Instead of feeling banished, Netanyahu took to his new position with gusto. He had long considered an economically strong Israel to be a necessary part of a secure Israel. For Netanyahu, that meant moving the Israeli economy into a more American-style free market. As it stood in 2003, Israel's **public sector** was much larger than Israel's **private sector**. Finance Minister Netanyahu described his greatest challenge as addressing "the huge mistake of establishing [Israel as] a socialist state."[3]

This time Netanyahu didn't try making deals to keep everyone happy, as he had disastrously done as prime minister. Instead, he made it clear from the start that everyone should prepare to make their own contributions to financial reforms.

He cut welfare spending, which had been thirty percent of the government's budget.[4] Those cuts included reducing income supplements to the middle class, as well as to the unemployed. As Netanyahu put it, "We will continue to push the unemployed to go to work, because that is the way to **eradicate** poverty."[5]

Netanyahu cut the budgets for government agencies, including small cuts to Israel's defense budget. No one had ever cut the defense budget before. He had the government sell off some of the companies it owned. Netanyahu also challenged the other main institutions he felt were holding back Israeli growth—the banks and unions. Through other reforms and tough negotiations, he reduced their power with the goal of increasing private competition among businesses. He also lowered the income taxes people had to pay.

Again, many people were upset with Netanyahu. People organized protests against his cuts in welfare spending. Unions went on strike. Banks tried to use their power to block reforms. This time, Netanyahu wasn't run out of office. There were two major differences between his time as prime minister and his time as finance minister: First, Netanyahu was largely successful in getting his reforms passed, despite the outcry. Second, his reforms worked.

Israel Gets through the Global Economic Crisis

In 2003, when Netanyahu became finance minister, the unemployment rate in Israel hit a high of nearly eleven percent.[6] It was cut almost in half in just five short years. The unemployment rate was down to nine percent by 2005, and dropped to six percent in 2008.[7] The country, which had been in recession from 2001 to 2003, enjoyed a **gross domestic product (GDP)** growth rate higher than six percent on average between 2004 and 2007.[8] Those were just some of the signs that the Israeli economy was growing strong.

In late 2008, much of the world was in a major economic crisis. Israel also suffered. Its unemployment rate started to creep up. Its GDP started to creep down. Even so, the strength of Israel's economy "made it one of the last countries to enter recession and among the earliest to exit."[9] Israel's GDP growth since 2009 continues to be higher than the global average.[10] The general consensus is that Netanyahu's financial reforms, which brought financial discipline to the government and spurred the private sector, were an important part of the reason why Israel came through the global recession so well.

Netanyahu Resigns

While Netanyahu was pushing through his economic reforms that angered so many people at the time, he was also feeling angry. In December 2003, Sharon had announced that Israel would withdraw from Gaza, a small strip of land to Israel's southwest that is heavily populated with Arabs. Like many people on the right, Netanyahu was strongly opposed to withdrawal. He argued that leaving Gaza was too great a security threat to Israel, and abandoning that land would make Gaza a launching pad for terror into Israel. It would also require the physical removal of the Jews who were currently living there. This was a painful event Israel had suffered before when it removed Jews living in the Sinai as part of the peace treaty it signed with Egypt in 1979.

Netanyahu resigned from the government in protest on August 7, 2005, when Sharon's cabinet approved the first phase of "disengagement," as the Gaza withdrawal plan was called. In his resignation letter, he wrote that the disengagement plan was against Likud's principles, it endangered Israel's security, and it threatened to "split the people."[11]

START-UP NATION

Israel got the nickname "Start-up Nation" after a book by the same name,[12] which sought to explain why the tiny nation surrounded by enemies has such an exciting business sector. Despite being founded as a socialist country, the Israeli population has a strong free-market mentality. It is a small nation, only slightly larger than New Jersey, and has roughly 8 million citizens. Even so, it generally ranks as one of the world's most economically competitive nations. Many of the world's most interesting technology advances have come from Israel, such as the first instant messaging program created during the early years of the Internet and a popular navigation application recently bought by Google.

Israel's record of creativity attracts companies and investors from around the world. There are many reasons for Israel's strong economy and vibrant business sector. Israel has a highly educated population, especially in the sciences. Credit is also given to the Israeli military. Most of Israel's citizens serve in the military, which fosters self-confidence, a willingness to take risks, and the ability to solve problems with limited resources. The combination of these qualities results in a high number of people with new ideas and the gumption to try them out.

Tel Aviv is Israel's largest city. Three of its most famous buildings make up Azrieli Center, a complex of offices and major shopping mall.

Tzipi Livni began her political career as a member of the Likud, holding various ministerial positions under Prime Minister Ariel Sharon and as Minister of Justice under Netanyahu from 2013–2014. After leaving politics for a short while, she founded the Hatnua party in 2012. Hatnua joined forces with the left-wing Labor party from the Zionist Union to oppose Likud and Netanyahu in the 2015 elections. Prior to politics, Livni was a lieutenant in the IDF, Mossad agent, and earned a law degree.

CHAPTER 6
MEET THE NEW PRIME MINISTER—Almost the Same as the Old Prime Minister

Can a politician win and lose the same election? In Israel, the answer is "yes." Israelis voted for a new Knesset on February 9, 2009. When the votes were counted, the Likud, again led by Netanyahu, had won twenty-seven of the Knesset's one hundred twenty seats. That more than doubled their seat count from before the election. However, the *Kadima* (kah-DEE-mah) party, lead by Tzipi Livni (TZIH-pee LIV-nee) had won twenty-eight seats. Now that Israel was no longer voting directly for the prime minister, it was the duty of the president to ask a party leader to form a government, or ruling coalition.

Normally, the president asks the leader of the party that has won the most seats to form the government. Prior to those elections, then Prime Minister Ehud Olmert resigned because he was the subject of criminal investigations. Livni became the new leader of the Kadima party, which had the most Knesset seats. As a result, President Shimon Peres asked Livni to form a new government coalition when Olmert resigned in September 2008. It was Livni's inability to form a government that was the reason Israel was having elections in the first place.

So for the first time in Israel's history, the president *didn't* ask the winning party's leader to form a government that February. Instead, he asked the leader of the party with the second highest percentage of the vote—Netanyahu.

Becoming Leader Again

Before Netanyahu could become prime minister again, he first had to become leader of the party again. Many on the right and in the Likud were as angry with Sharon over the Gaza disengagement as Netanyahu. In September 2005, Netanyahu pushed for a party primary so the Likud could elect a new leader. That effort failed. Even so, Sharon left the Likud on November 21, 2005 to form the Kadima (the Hebrew word for "forward") party with former members from both the Likud and the Labor parties.

Now with no party leader, the Likud held its primary. In a crowded field of candidates, Netanyahu returned to lead the Likud with forty-four percent of the vote. His nearest competitor

Netanyahu casts his vote on February 10, 2009. Despite the Likud coming in second in the popular vote, Israeli president Shimon Peres tasked Netanyahu with forming the new government. This election marks Netanyahu's return to the prime minister's office since he lost the election to Ehud Barak in 1999.

won just thirty-three percent.[1] Netanyahu, as the party's new leader, remained in the Knesset as head of the opposition until the 2009 election. On March 31, 2009, Netanyahu was sworn in as prime minister for the second time.

Big Issues

The challenges of being an Israeli prime minister still remained. A few months after being sworn in, Netanyahu gave a speech at an Israeli university in which he expressed support, for the first time, to the idea of a two state solution for Israelis and Palestinians to live side by side in peace. Netanyahu believed that the Israeli people had "achieved a wide national consensus on the idea of two states for two peoples."[2]

In the years since this speech, increasing areas of land in the Middle East have come under the control of Islamic extremists from which they attack local populations. As a result, Netanyahu stated in 2015 that he thinks "anyone who is going to establish a Palestinian state today and evacuate lands is giving attack grounds to the radical Islam against the state of Israel."[3] His opponents accuse him of abandoning the two-state solution. Netanyahu and his advocates say this isn't so. Instead, they say that withdrawal from further lands under current conditions would result in greater danger for Israel, not peace.

The more immediate concern for Netanyahu was whether Iran had a nuclear weapon. Netanyahu described Iran as the "greatest threat not just to Israel and the Middle East but to civilization."[4] Netanyahu has said that Israel will make a military strike on Iran's nuclear facilities if necessary for the security of Israel. During the Knesset election campaign in March 2015, Netanyahu addressed a joint session of the US Congress arguing that the Obama Administration's positions in current negotiations with Iran would leave Iran empowered to

Peace talks in Sharm El Sheikh, Egypt on September 14, 2010. Hosted by Egyptian president Hosni Mubarak (second from right), Netanyahu is joined by US Secretary of State Hillary Clinton and Palestinian president Mahmoud Abbas.

eventually build a nuclear weapon. While there is agreement between Israel's left and right that Iran is a strategic threat to country, Israeli politicians from the left criticized Netanyahu's speech for making disagreements with the United States so public.

The Israelis aren't optimistic about these two big issues. The majority of Israeli Jews want to have peace talks with the Palestinians, but they don't expect talks to lead to peace.[5] Nearly two-thirds of Israeli Jews believe that Palestinian leadership isn't ready to make peace regardless of whether Israel is led by a right-wing or left-wing government.[6]

A majority also see a nuclear Iran as a threat to their country's very existence,[7] but they're split on whether Israel should attack Iran alone.[8] Israelis didn't believe a previous agreement between Iran, the United States, and other world powers, would cause Iran to stop its nuclear program.[9] Sixty-one percent of Israeli Jews are concerned that the Obama Administration will agree to a new Iran deal even if Israel makes it clear that it believes the terms put Israel at risk.[10]

Netanyahu, standing with Ehud Barak, holds up an operations manual for C-704 anti-ship missiles written in Farsi, the language spoken in Iran. The manual was part of the evidence seized by Israel from the ship "Victoria" in 2011. The Victoria had been loaded in the Syrian port of Latakia just two weeks after Iranian ships had docked at the same port. The Israeli navy seized the ship and its cargo of weaponry, which it believed was to be delivered to terror organizations in Gaza. Israel had earlier seized another ship delivering 500 tons of weapons, including rockets and grenades, from Iran to terror groups in Lebanon.

King Bibi

The result of the Israelis' consensus about their foreign relations is that there's been growing focus on domestic issues. Netanyahu's government almost stumbled over the issue of drafting **Haredim** (ha-RAY-deem), ultra-Orthodox Jews, into the IDF. There is broad agreement among non-Haredi Israelis that the number of religious exemptions from military duty should be greatly reduced. The vast majority of Israelis serve in the IDF, and they don't think it right that some Israelis don't share the burden.

On May 8, 2012, Netanyahu announced a national unity government. The Kadima party would join the governing

Inside an Israeli voting booth. Israelis vote for a political party, not a person. A voter selects the note that has her chosen party's letters and puts it in the envelope she received from the poll worker.

coalition, giving Netanyahu a supermajority of ninety-four of the Knesset's one hundred twenty seats. No Israeli prime minister had ever lead a coalition so large. When Netanyahu announced the national unity government, he was called "King Bibi" and "King of Israel" in the press. All the parties in the coalition agreed the draft exemption for the Haredim had to end. They couldn't agree on how to do it. The supermajority coalition broke apart within two months.

With a smaller, politically weakened coalition, Netanyahu couldn't get support for his proposed 2013 budget. As a result, he called for early elections. At the time he called for elections, polls showed that "King Bibi" had no serious rivals even though the Israeli public was evenly split on the question of whether they were satisfied with his performance.[11] That election, held January 22, 2013, focused mainly on domestic issues. In addition to the issue of a universal military draft, Israelis were concerned

Netanyahu meets US president Barack Obama at Ben Gurion Airport on March 20, 2013. This was President Obama's first trip to Israel since taking office. One of the purposes of the trip was to improve the personal relations between Netanyahu and Obama, which had been strained. However, the relationship between the two leaders continues to decline, most recently regarding disagreements over Iran's nuclear program.

Netanyahu and US Secretary of Defense Chuck Hagel issue a joint press statement on May 16, 2014. As part of Hagel's trip to Israel, he visited the tombs of Theodor Herzl, the founder of political Zionism, and Prime Minister Yitzhak Rabin, who was assassinated by an Israeli Jew in 1995. Both men, along with other Israeli presidents and prime ministers, are buried at Mount Herzl in Jerusalem. Mount Herzl is Israel's national cemetery.

The Knesset building in Jerusalem. Israel's Knesset has 120 members to mirror the 120 members of the Knesset HaGedolah (ki-neh-set ha-geh-DOH-lah) or "Great Assembly," first organized in Israel during the sixth century BCE. The members of the Knesset HaGedolah were the religious leaders of the Jewish community who finalized many Jewish religious texts, wrote prayers, and handed down religious laws.

One of Likud's campaign tents during the March 2015 elections. The posters show the Likud's campaign slogan: "It's us or them. Only Likud. Only Netanyahu." The slogan was in response to the Zionist Union's campaign slogan "It's us or him," a reference to Netanyahu.

Netanyahu and Isaac Herzog, the leader of the Zionist Union party along with Tzipi Livni, share some television time just two days prior to the March 2015 election. The two party leaders didn't have a formal debate during the campaign, but had a "mini-debate" when their interview times on an Israeli news program overlapped.

about the high cost of living in the country and reforming its election laws. The election also turned out more difficult for Netanyahu than first expected. His Likud party, joined by another right wing, security-minded party, still won the highest number of seats by far, but it was also far fewer seats than it had had.

In December 2014, Netanyahu called for new elections due to political fights with Likud's center-party coalition partner. Likud's, and Netanyahu's, main rival was a merger of left-wing parties under a new party name, Zionist Union. During the election, the Zionist Union and center party Yesh Atid again focused on domestic issues, particularly the increasing cost of living in Israel. Netanyahu and Likud focused on security. Polls during the campaign showed either that Likud and Zionist Union would win a similar amount of seats, or that the Zionist Union would win more, thus removing Netanyahu as prime minister. In the end, Likud won the election in a landslide, nearly doubling its number of seats in the Knesset from eighteen to thirty. The Zionist Union won twenty-four seats.

So at sixty-five years old, finally a zakayn, Netanyahu will likely retain his position as prime minister. He has now been Israel's prime minister for more than nine years.

Netanyahu still has plenty of critics. Critics on the right haven't forgotten that Netanyahu gave away Hebron to the Palestinians and they worry he'll give away too much in future negotiations. Critics on the left believe Netanyahu's singular focus on Iran distracts from other important issues, like the peace process with the Palestinians and domestic social issues. Others worry that such a lack of leadership alternatives is unhealthy for a democracy. But for now, the "King of Israel" remains, working to defend Israel's security. Any father would be proud.

MEIR DAGAN

He's been called "the last man in Israel to stand up to Benjamin Netanyahu."[12] Meir Dagan was the head of the Mossad, Israel's spy agency, from 2002 through 2011. Under his leadership, the Mossad increased its budget, its technology, and its operations abroad. So Dagan is known as a pretty tough guy.

He is highly critical of Netanyahu's handling of Iran and its program to develop nuclear weapons. Dagan has some experience with the nuclear issue. During his leadership of Mossad, the agency developed information that Syria was building a nuclear reactor. The IDF then destroyed the Syrian reactor with an airstrike in 2007. It is also believed (although it isn't confirmed) that the Mossad, under Dagan, took many actions against Iran's nuclear program. Some of those actions included releasing the Stuxnet virus, which damaged the software used by Iran's reactors and getting Iran to buy defective equipment.

When Dagan left his post, he began to criticize Netanyahu publicly about his Iran policy. Dagan suggests that Netanyahu may be too quick to push a military attack on Iran. He believes a military strike too soon would make matters worse. In his view, a military strike on Iran wouldn't stop that country's nuclear program because there are too many nuclear facilities throughout Iran; however, a premature strike would, Dagan says, start a regional war.

The ultimate goal, according to Dagan, should be to support democratic elements in Iran as they work to free themselves from the control of the **mullahs**. In the meantime, Dagan says the world should put greater economic and diplomatic pressure on Iran. In his opinion, this type of increased pressure on Iran can prevent the need for an Israeli military strike.

Dagan receives recognition in 2011 as he leaves the Mossad, from the Chief of General Staff of the IDF, on behalf of IDF soldiers and commanders. The certificate represents the tree planted in Dagan's honor by the Jewish National Fund.

TIMELINE

1903   Netanyahu's grandfather, Rabbi Natan Mileikowsky, attends the Sixth Zionist Congress.

1920   Rabbi Mileikowsky settles in Tzfat, a town in the north of Mandatory Palestine.

1948   The state of Israel is formally re-established on its ancient homeland.

1949   Benjamin Netanyahu is born in Tel Aviv on October 21.

1967   Netanyahu enters the Israel Defense Force (IDF).

1972   Netanyahu is discharged from the IDF and begins studying at the Massachusetts Institute of Technology (MIT) in the United States.

1976   Netanyahu works at the Boston Consulting Group. His brother Yonatan (Yoni or Jonathan) is killed on July 4.

1978   Netanyahu heads the Jonathan Institute for Peace.

1980   Netanyahu works at Rim Industries.

1982   Netanyahu is appointed Deputy Chief of Mission, serving under Israel's ambassador to the United States, Moshe Arens.

1984   Netanyahu is appointed Israel's ambassador to the United Nations.

1988   Netanyahu returns to Israel and is elected to the Knesset as a member of the Likud Party. He serves as Deputy Minister of Foreign Affairs under Prime Minister Yitzhak Shamir until 1991.

1993   Netanyahu gets elected as chairman of the Likud Party.

1996   Netanyahu gets elected prime minister of Israel.

1999   Ehud Barak, Netanyahu's former commander in the Sayeret Matkal, defeats Netanyahu in elections for prime minister.

2002   Netanyahu is appointed Minister of Foreign Affairs under Prime Minister Ariel Sharon.

2003   Prime Minister Sharon removes Netanyahu as minister of Foreign Affairs and appoints him minister of Finance.

2005   Netanyahu resigns as finance minister in protest of Sharon's Gaza withdrawal. Sharon leaves the Likud Party to start the centrist Kadima Party, and Netanyahu gets re-elected head of Likud.

2009   President Shimon Peres selects Netanyahu to form a government coalition after the elections, despite the Likud party coming in second in the voting. Netanyahu is sworn in as prime minister and gives a speech endorsing a two-state solution.

2012   Netanyahu calls for elections; his Likud Party joins with another right wing political party, Beiteinu.

2013   Likud-Beiteinu wins thirty-one seats in the election and the highest percentage of votes; Netanyahu is sworn in as prime minister for the third time.

2014   Netanyahu calls for a national unity government in the wake of increased terror attacks on Israelis in Jerusalem.

2015   The Likud wins an unexpected and crushing victory in elections, paving the way for Netanyahu to start his third consecutive term as prime minister.

CHAPTER NOTES

Introduction

1. Rafael Medoff, "Benzion Netanyahu's role in U.S. politics," *Jewish Telegraphic Agency*, April 30, 2012, http://www.jta.org/2012/04/30/news-opinion/politics/benzion-netanyahus-role-in-u-s-politics

Chapter 1: Growing Up Netanyahu

1. "Call him prime minister, but never 'Bibi'," *Jweekly.com*, June 21, 1996, http://www.jweekly.com/article/full/3511/call-him-prime-minister-but-never-bibi/

2. Melanie Lidman, "PM was 'responsible' sixth-grader, evaluation shows," *The Jerusalem Post*, August 28, 2012, http://www.jpost.com/National-News/PM-was-responsible-sixth-grader-evaluation-shows

3. Charles H. Ball, "Professor recalls Netanyahu's intense studies in three fields," *MIT News*, June 5, 1996, http://web.mit.edu/newsoffice/1996/netanyahu-0605.html

4. Richard Stengel, "Will He Make War? Will He Make Peace?" *Time*, May 28, 2012, http://content.time.com/time/magazine/article/0,9171,2115042,00.html

5. Mitch Ginsburg, "Saving Sergeant Netanyahu," *The Times of Israel*, October 25, 2012, http://www.timesofisrael.com/saving-sergeant-netanyahu/

6. Yossi Klein-Halevi, "The Savior—How Bibi Netanyahu salvaged the Israeli right," *New Republic*, June 21, 1993, 20. http://www.unz.org/Pub/NewRepublic-1993jun21

7. Benjamin Netanyahu and Iddo Netanyahu, eds. *The Letters of Jonathan Netanyahu: The Commander of the Entebbe Rescue Force*. Jerusalem, Israel: Geffen Publishing House, 2001, xiii.

Chapter 2: A Scholar and A Soldier

1. Charles H. Ball, "Professor recalls Netanyahu's intense studies in three fields," http://web.mit.edu/newsoffice/1996/netanyahu-0605.html

2. Joshua Mitnick, "Israel's Calculus on Iran: Shaped by leaders' youth in daring commando unit?" *Christian Science Monitor*, March 4, 2012, http://www.csmonitor.com/World/Middle-East/2012/0304/Israel-s-calculus-on-Iran-Shaped-by-leaders-youth-in-daring-commando-unit

Chapter 3: Entering Politics

1. Richard Stengel, "Will He Make War? Will He Make Peace?" http://content.time.com/time/magazine/article/0,9171,2115042,00.html

Chapter 4: Netanyahu's First Try

1. Neill Lochery, "The Netanyahu Era: From Crisis to Crisis, 1996–1999," *Israel: The First Hundred Years: Volume II: From War to Peace?* New York: Frank Cass Publishers, 2000, 231.

2. Efraim Torgovnik, "The Centre Party," *Israel at the Polls*, 1999, vol. 3, London: Frank Cass Publishers, 2001, 143.

Chapter 5: Returning to Politics

1. "Netanyahu weighs Israeli election challenge." *CNN.* December 4, 2000, http://www.cnn.com.br/2000/WORLD/meast/12/04/mideast.netanyahu.reut/

2. Israel Ministry of Foreign Affairs: "Elections February 2001—Special Update," MFA.gov, February 20, 2001, http://mfa.gov.il/MFA/AboutIsrael/History/Pages/Elections%20February%202001%20-%20Special%20Update.aspx

3. Mati Wagner, "Israel's Capitalist Election," *Commentary*, March 1, 2013: 23. https://www.commentarymagazine.com/article/israels-capitalist-election/

4. Kimberley A. Strassel, "Israel Gets a Taste of Friedman," *The Wall Street Journal*, March 1, 2004, http://online.wsj.com/articles/SB107810224039142434

5. Greg Myre, "Netanyahu Gets Tough to Transform Israel's Economy." *New York Times*, October 24, 2004: A18, http://www.nytimes.com/2004/10/24/international/middleeast/24mideast.html?pagewanted=print&position=&_r=0

6. "Historical Data Graphs per Year—Unemployment rate—Israel," IndexMundi, http://www.indexmundi.com/g/g.aspx?c=is&v=74

7. Ibid.

8. Organization for Economic Co-operation and Development (OECD): "Israel: Review of the Financial System," *oecd.org*, September 2011: 8, http://www.oecd.org/finance/financial-markets/49497958.pdf

9. "Beyond the start-up nation," *The Economist*, December 29, 2010, http://www.economist.com/node/17796932

10. Economist Intelligence Unit: "Israel Country Report January 2014,": 12, Economist.com, http://www.economist.com/topics/israel

11. Yossi Verter Haaretz, "Netanyahu quits government over disengagement." *Haaretz*, August 7, 2005, http://www.haaretz.com/news/netanyahu-quits-government-over-disengagement-1.166110

12. Daniel Senor and Saul Singer, *Start-up Nation: The Story of Israel's Economic Miracle*. New York: Twelve, 2009.

Chapter 6: MEET THE NEW PRIME MINISTER—Almost the Same as the Old Prime Minister

1. Ken Ellingwood, "Sharon Is Fine After Stroke, Doctors Say," *Los Angeles Times*, December 20, 2005, http://articles.latimes.com/2005/dec/20/world/fg-sharon20

2. Barak Ravid, "Netanyahu: We have consensus on two-state solution," *Haaretz*, July 5, 2009, http://www.haaretz.com/news/netanyahu-we-have-consensus-on-two-state-solution-1.279374

3. Eli Lake. "Israel Chose Bibi Over Barack," *Bloomberg View*, March 18, 2015, http://www.bloombergview.com/articles/2015-03-18/israel-chose-bibi-over-barack

4. Richard Stengel, "Will He Make War? Will He Make Peace?" http://content.time.com/time/magazine/article/0,9171,2115042,00.html

5. The Israel Democracy Institute, Tel Aviv University: "The Peace Index – September 2013," http://en.idi.org.il/media/2733007/Peace%20Index%20September%202013.pdf

6. The Israel Democracy Institute, Tel Aviv University, "The Peace Index – February 2015," http://en.idi.org.il/media/3930815/Peace_Index_February_2015-Eng.pdf

7. *Jerusalem Post*, "65% of Israelis say no danger of new Holocaust," March 3, 2013, http://www.jpost.com/Israel/65-percent-of-Israelis-say-no-danger-of-new-Holocaust-308529

8. *Israel Hayom*, "Poll: Israelis don't believe Iran will stop its nuclear program," November 25, 2013, http://www.israelhayom.com/site/newsletter_article.php?id=13561

9. Ibid.

10. The Israel Democracy Institute, Tel Aviv University, "The Peace Index – January 2015," http://en.idi.org.il/media/3875193/Peace_Index_January_2015-Eng.pdf

11. Yossi Verter, "Haaretz poll: Netanyahu beats election rivals, right-wing bloc grows stronger," *Haaretz*, November 10, 2012, http://www.haaretz.com/news/national/haaretz-poll-netanyahu-beats-election-rivals-right-wing-bloc-grows-stronger.premium-1.469240

12. Kedar Pavgi, "The FP Top 100 Global Thinkers," *Foreign Policy*, November 28, 2011, http://www.foreignpolicy.com/articles/2011/11/28/the_fp_top_100_global_thinkers

WORKS CONSULTED

———. "65% of Israelis say no danger of new Holocaust." *Jerusalem Post*. April 3, 2013. http://www.jpost.com/Israel/65-percent-of-Israelis-say-no-danger-of-new-Holocaust-308529

Ajami, Fouad. "A hard reckoning with peace." *U.S. News & World Report*. November 1998. 125 No. 18: 38. http://connection.ebscohost.com/c/articles/1227533/hard-reckoning-peace

Alpert, Zalman. "The Maggid Of Netanyahu." *Zionist Organization of America*. April 29, 2009. http://zoa.org/2009/04/102450-the-maggid-of-netanyahu/

Associated Press. "Bougie, Bibi and Ghandi: A guide to Israeli politicians' weird nicknames." *Haaretz*. December 3, 2013. http://www.haaretz.com/news/features/1.561480

Ball, Charles H. "Professor recalls Netanyahu's intense studies in three fields." *MIT News*. June 5, 1996. http://web.mit.edu/newsoffice/1996/netanyahu-0605.html

Beyer, Lisa. "Israel: The Making of Benjamin Netanyahu." *Time*. June 10, 1996. http://topics.time.com/benjamin-netanyahu/articles/6/

———. "Beyond the start-up nation." *The Economist*. January 1, 2011. http://www.economist.com/node/17769932

———. "Call him prime minister, but never 'Bibi'." *Jweekly.com*. June 21, 1996. http://www.jweekly.com/article/full/3511/call-him-prime-minister-but-never-bibi/

———. "Elections February 2001—Special Update." *Israel Ministry of Foreign Affairs*. http://mfa.gov.il/MFA/AboutIsrael/History/Pages/Elections%20February%202001%20-%20Special%20Update.aspx

Duek, Nehama. "Ex-ambassadors urge Netanyahu to cut speech," *Ynet News Magazine*, February 13, 2015. http://www.ynetnews.com/articles/0,7340,L-4626374,00.html

Ellingwood, Ken. "Sharon Is Fine After Stroke, Doctors Say." *Los Angeles Times*. December 20, 2005. http://articles.latimes.com/2005/dec/20/world/fg-sharon20

Feith, Douglas J. "A Strategy for Israel." *Commentary*. September 1997. http://www.dougfeith.com/docs/1997_09_Feith_Commentary_A_Strategy_for_Israel.pdf

Ginsburg, Mitch. "Saving Sergeant Netanyahu." *The Times of Israel*. October 25, 2012. http://www.timesofisrael.com/saving-sergeant-netanyahu/

Goldberg, J.J. "Israel's Houdini." *Commonweal*. 126 No. 7: 9. April 9, 1999.

Haaretz. "Netanyahu and Herzog spar on Jerusalem, Iran," March 14, 2015. http://www.haaretz.com/news/israel-election-2015/1.646878

Haaretz, Yossi Verter. "Haaretz poll: Netanyahu beats election rivals, right-wing bloc grows stronger." *Haaretz*. November 10, 2012. http://www.haaretz.com/news/national/haaretz-poll-netanyahu-beats-election-rivals-right-wing-bloc-grows-stronger.premium-1.469240

Haaretz, Yossi Verter. "Netanyahu quits government over disengagement." *Haaretz*. August 7, 2005. http://www.haaretz.com/news/netanyahu-quits-government-over-disengagement-1.166110

"Historical Data Graphs per Year—Unemployment rate—Israel." *IndexMundi*. n.d. http://www.indexmundi.com/g/g.aspx?c=is&v=74

———. "Israel." *Central Intelligence Agency. The World Factbook*. https://www.cia.gov/library/publications/the-world-factbook/geos/is.html

———. "Israel Country Report January 2014." *Economist Intelligence Unit*. http://www.economist.com/topics/israel

———. "Israeli Election Results—May 1996." *Israel Ministry of Foreign Affairs*. http://mfa.gov.il/MFA/AboutIsrael/History/Pages/Israeli%20Election%20Results-%20May%201996.aspx

———. "Israeli Election Results—May 1999." *Israel Ministry of Foreign Affairs*. http://mfa.gov.il/MFA/AboutIsrael/History/Pages/Israeli%20Election%20Results-%20May%201999.aspx

Hoffman, Gil. "Former PM Shamir passes away at age 96 in Tel Aviv," *The Jerusalem Post*, June 30, 2012. http://www.jpost.com/National-News/Former-PM-Shamir-passes-away-at-age-96-in-Tel-Aviv

———. "Likud's lead over Zionist Union falls from four seats to one." *The Jerusalem Post*, February 13, 2015, http://www.jpost.com/Israel-Elections/Obama-interfering-in-Israeli-election-according-to-Jerusalem-Post-poll-390925

Horovitz, David. "King Bibi and his divided people," *The Times of Israel*, March 18, 2015, http://www.timesofisrael.com/king-bibi-and-his-divided-people/

IDF website. "A look back at Operation Isotope," http://www.idf.il/1283-18936-en/Dover.aspx

Katz, Samuel M. *Targeting Terror: Counterterrorist Raids*. Minneapolis, MN: Lerner Publishing, 2004.

WORKS CONSULTED

Kershner, Isabel. "Netanyahu Fires Ministers and Calls for Elections," *The New York Times*. December 2, 2014, http://www.nytimes.com/2014/12/03/world/middleeast/israel-netanyahu-cabinet-elections.html?_r=0

Klein-Halevi, Yossi. "The Savior." *New Republic*. June 21, 1993: 20. http://www.unz.org/Pub/NewRepublic-1993jun21

Knesset. "Binyamin (Bibi) Netanyahu—Biography." http://www.knesset.gov.il/elections/pm/ebio_pm_4.htm

Kredo, Alan and John Tabin. "Tempers Flare in Israel at Key Debate," *The Washington Free Beacon*, March 16, 2015, http://freebeacon.com/politics/in-israel-hostility-and-tempers-flare-at-key-debate/

Lidman, Melanie. "PM was 'responsible' sixth-grader, evaluation shows." *The Jerusalem Post*. August 28, 2012. http://www.jpost.com/National-News/PM-was-responsible-sixth-grader-evaluation-shows

Lochery, Neill. "The Netanyahu Era: From Crisis to Crisis, 1996—1999." *Israel: The First Hundred Years: Volume II: From War to Peace?* New York: Frank Cass Publishers, 2000.

Medoff, Rafael. "Benzion Netanyahu's role in U.S. politics." *Jewish Telegraphic Agency*. April 30, 2012. http://www.jta.org/2012/04/30/news-opinion/politics/benzion-netanyahus-role-in-u-s-politics

Miller, Stephan. "Likud-Beytenu jumps 15 seats in new poll." *Times of Israel*. January 23, 2014. http://www.timesofisrael.com/likud-beytenu-jumps-15-seats-in-new-poll/

Mitnick, Joshua. "Israel's Calculus on Iran: Shaped by leaders' youth in daring commando unit?" *Christian Science Monitor*. March 4, 2012. http://www.csmonitor.com/World/Middle-East/2012/0304/Israel-s-calculus-on-Iran-Shaped-by-leaders-youth-in-daring-commando-unit

Myre, Greg. "In Israel, Opposition Rises to Netanyahu's Austerity Moves." *The New York Times*. April 1, 2003. http://www.nytimes.com/2003/04/01/world/in-israel-opposition-rises-to-netanyahu-s-austerity-moves.html

Myre, Greg. "Israel's Steps to Stem Economic Slide Draw Praise and Protests." *The New York Times*. July 20, 2003. http://www.nytimes.com/2003/07/20/world/israel-s-steps-to-stem-economic-slide-draw-praise-and-protests.html

Myre, Greg. "Netanyahu Gets Tough to Transform Israel's Economy." *New York Times*. October 24, 2004. http://www.nytimes.com/2004/10/24/international/middleeast/24mideast.html?pagewanted=print&position=&_r=0

Naor, Arye. "Hawks' Beaks Doves' Feathers Likud Prime Ministers Between Ideology and Reality." *Israel Studies*, September, 2005. 10 No. 3: 154-191.

Netanyahu, Benjamin and Iddo Netanyahu, eds. *The Letters of Jonathan Netanyahu: The Commander of the Entebbe Rescue Force*. Jerusalem, Israel: Geffen Publishing House, 2001.

———. "Netanyahu weighs Israeli election challenge." *CNN*. December 4, 2000. http://edition.cnn.com/2000/WORLD/meast/12/04/mideast.netanyahu.reut/

Organization for Economic Co-operation and Development (OECD). "Israel: Review of the Financial System." *oecd.org*. September 2011: 8. http://www.oecd.org/finance/financial-markets/49497958.pdf

Pavgi, Kedar. "The FP Top 100 Global Thinkers." *Foreign Policy*. November 28, 2011. http://www.foreignpolicy.com/articles/2011/11/28/the_fp_top_100_global_thinkers

———. "Poll: Israelis don't believe Iran will stop its nuclear program." *Israel Hayom*. November 25, 2013. http://www.israelhayom.com/site/newsletter_article.php?id=13561

———. "Poll reveals that Israelis support Netanyahu and are frustrated by Lapid." *Middle East Monitor*. October 18, 2013. https://www.middleeastmonitor.com/news/middle-east/7853-poll-reveals-that-israelis-support-netanyahu-and-are-frustrated-by-lapid

———. "Prime Minister Benjamin Netanyahu." *Prime Ministers' Office*. http://www.pmo.gov.il/English/PrimeMinister/Pages/PrimeMinister-CurriculumVitae.aspx

Ravid, Barak. "Netanyahu: We have consensus on two-state solution." *Haaretz*. July 5, 2009. http://www.haaretz.com/news/netanyahu-we-have-consensus-on-two-state-solution-1.279374

Remnick, David. "The Vegetarian." *New Yorker*. September 3, 2012. http://www.newyorker.com/magazine/2012/09/03/the-vegetarian

Rudoren, Jodi. "Unity Government in Israel Disbanding Over Dispute on Draft." *The New York Times*. July 17, 2012. http://www.nytimes.com/2012/07/18/world/middleeast/unity-government-in-israel-disbanding-over-dispute-on-draft.html?_r=0

WORKS CONSULTED

Senor, Daniel and Saul Singer. *Start-up Nation: The Story of Israel's Economic Miracle*. New York: Twelve, 2009.

Sheizaf, Noam. "The Triumph of the Far Right in Israel." *The Nation*. January 28, 2013: 6-8. http://www.thenation.com/article/172102/triumph-far-right-israel#

Shlaim, Avi. *The Iron Wall: Israel and the Arab World*. New York: W.W. Norton & Company, 2001.

Simpson, David and Josh Levs. "Israeli PM Netanyahu: Iran nuclear deal 'historic mistake.'" *CNN*. November 25, 2013. http://edition.cnn.com/2013/11/24/world/meast/iran-israel/

Stengel, Richard."Will He Make War? Will He Make Peace?" *Time*. May 28, 2012. http://content.time.com/time/magazine/article/0,9171,2115042,00.html

Sonsino, Iddan. "Sayeret Matkal veteran recounts Sabena operation, 40 years later." *Israel Defense Forces*. May 13, 2012. http://www.idf.il/1283-15939-en/Dover.asp

Strassel, Kimberley A. "Israel Gets a Taste of Friedman." *The Wall Street Journal*. March 1, 2004. http://online.wsj.com/articles/SB10781022403914243

———. "The Peace Index—October 2013." *The Israel Democracy Institute, Tel Aviv University*. http://www.peaceindex.org/files/Peace%20Index%20Data%20-%20October%202013%20-%20Eng.pdf

———. "The Spymaster: Meir Dagan on Iran's Threat." *CBS News*. YouTube. http://www.youtube.com/watch?v=qi6YDTC0Rb4

Torgovnik, Efraim. "The Centre Party," *Israel at the Poll, 1999*. London: Frank Cass Publishers, 2001: 3.

Wagner, Mati. "Israel's Capitalist Election." *Commentary*. March 2013: 23. https://www.commentarymagazine.com/article/israels-capitalist-election/

Wilkinson, Stephan. "Seven Most Daring Raids Ever." *EBSCO Host Connection*. October/November 2009: 39. http://connection.ebscohost.com/c/articles/44204197/seven-most-daring-raids-ever

Williams, Armstrong. "Conversations with Netanyahu." *Townhall.com*. September 4, 2003. http://townhall.com/columnists/armstrongwilliams/2003/09/04/conversations_with_netanyahu/page/full

Zonszein, Mairav. "Anyone But Netanyahu?" *The Nation,* March 16, 2015. http://www.thenation.com/article/201553/anyone-netanyahu#

FURTHER READING

Greenfeld, Howard. *A Promise Fulfilled: Theodor Herzl, Chaim Weizmann, David Ben-Gurion, and the Creation of the State of Israel*. New York: Greenwillow, 2005.

Gurko, Miriam. *Theodor Herzl, the Road to Israel*. Philadelphia: Jewish Publication Society, 1989.

Miklowitz, Gloria D. *Masada: The Last Fortress*. Grand Rapids, MI: William B. Eerdmans Publishing Company, 1999.

Stone, Tanya. *Ilan Ramon: Israel's First Astronaut*. Minneapolis: Millbrook Press, 2003.

Warren, Andrea. *Surviving Hitler: A Boy in the Nazi Death Camps*. New York: HarperCollins, 2002.

SELECTED WORKS BY BENJAMIN NETANYAHU

Netanyahu, Benjamin. *A Place Among the Nations*. New York: Bantam, 1993; re-titled *A Durable Peace: Israel and Its Place Among the Nations*. New York: Bantam, 2000.

Netanyahu, Benjamin. *Fighting Terrorism: How Democracies Can Defeat Domestic and International Terrorism*. New York: Farrar Straus & Giroux, 1995.

ON THE INTERNET

Benjamin Netanyahu
    http://www.biography.com/people/benjamin-netanyahu-9421908
Israel Fights Arab Nations in Yom Kippur War, speech by Abba Eban, 1973
    http://www.history.com/speeches/israel-fights-arab-nations-in-yom-kippur-war#israel-fights-arab-nations-in-yom-kippur-war
Israeli Prime Ministers
    http://www.akhlah.com/israel/government/prime-ministers/
Zionism
    http://encyclopedia.kids.net.au/page/zi/Zionism

GLOSSARY

anti-semitism (an-tee SEH-mi-tiz-uhm)—discrimination against or hatred of Jews

coalition (COH-a-lih-shun)—an alliance or agreement between political parties, often temporary

Deputy Chief of Mission—title given to the diplomat who is second in command at an embassy or other diplomatic mission

eradicate (eh-RAI-dih-kayt)—remove

Eretz Yisrael (eh-RETZ yis-RAH-el)—Hebrew for the "land of Israel;" used to refer to all of Israel within its biblical boundaries

gross domestic product (GDP)—the total value of a nation's goods and services, measured in dollars, generally used to rank the health and size of a nation's economy

Haredim (ha-RAY-deem)—Hebrew for "trembles," umbrella term used to refer to ultra-Orthodox Jews

mullah—title given to an Islamic religious teacher or leader

national unity government—name given for a ruling coalition made up of the major parties that are political rivals; it creates a super-majority in the parliament and is typically formed during times of national crisis

Palestinian Authority (PA)—the governing entity of the Palestinians. It oversees the administration of Palestinian-controlled areas of the West Bank

private sector—part of the economy not controlled by government

public sector— services and jobs provided by the government and funded by taxpayers

ruling coalition (also "government")—term used in a parliamentary system to describe the coalition of parties that has the majority of the seats in parliament

secular—term used in Israel to describe people who don't follow strict religious practices

Yom Kippur (YOWM kee-POOR)—the holiest Jewish holiday, observed by fasting and prayers of repentance

Zionism (ZIH-uh-ni-zum)—the philosophy that Jews should have an independent Jewish country in their native homeland

Zionist (ZIH-uh-nist)—a person or movement who believes in Zionism

INDEX

About the Author

Elisa Silverman has written a number of books on Israel for Mitchell Lane Publishers. Originally from Chicago, Elisa has lived and worked in Jerusalem, Israel for over a decade. Today, Elisa is a freelance marketing content writer, who also writes on legal and educational topics. She was graduated from Brandeis University with a bachelor's degree in philosophy, and holds a law degree from Emory University School of Law. You can follow Elisa on Twitter @ElisaKapha.